Perspectives of Nature
Volume 2

Perspectives of Nature Volume 2
ISBN: 978-1-945307-23-2

Copyright © 2020 by Paul Košir
First published March, 2020

With the exception of brief quotes for the purpose of review, no part of this book may be reproduced or utilized in any form or by any means, electronic or mechanical, without express written permission from the publisher.

Published by
Nature Works Publishing
1235 Denton Street
La Crosse, WI 54601
sciromanticpoetry@gmail.com

Book designed by Rodney Schroeter

Perspectives of Nature Volume 2

Scientifically Romantic and Experiential Nature Poetry

by Paul Košir

Acknowledgements

I must gratefully acknowledge
Rodney Schroeter,
whose confidence from the beginning
in my scientifically romantic style of poetry
made this project imaginable
and whose advice during the process
made the project achievable.

I also must gratefully acknowledge
the contributions to this work
of the members of the
La Crosse Area Writers Group,
and LAWG Poets,
who helped me to polish my good poems
into publishable works.

Finally, I must gratefully acknowledge
my wife, Lilly,
for her cheerful and helpful responses
to my frequent questions and complaints
while dealing ineffectively
with computer situations.

Author's Introduction

For more than two decades, I wrote no poems.
In my initial burst of nearly a dozen poems beginning in the late 1980s,
I wrote poetry that described the science behind natural phenomena and
processes. It was picturesque, instructive, and sometimes light hearted.
Early in 2012, I emerged from my dormancy with "Sun Dogs," a poem that
appears in my first collection, *Perspectives of Nature*. I wrote it to see if I still
was adept at writing poetry after time off as a father, teacher, naturalist, and
historian. It seemed I still had the knack, so I continued to write.

Most of my poems since "Sun Dogs," including many of those in *Perspectives
of Nature Volume 2,* use scientific terms. Definitions of more obscure terms
and infrequently-used words can be found on the left-hand page opposite the
poem in which the words or terms are found. These include terms that have
more familiar definitions in contexts other than science (e.g. "mantle" and
"murder"). They are listed in order of appearance in the associated poem.

Readers who purchase print editions of this booklet may want to use the
blank portions of the left-hand pages for journal entries.
These pages also could be used to record notes and observations in any of
the topics found in the poems. Locations of springs, finding an agate or
geode, visiting a mussel bed, listening to a frog chorus, observing spider web-
building, experiencing a thunderstorm, seeing fireflies,
and the arrival of Spring all are worthy entries.
Writing in this booklet would not ruin its leaves, but cause them to flower.

My verses accurately describe the natural world without romanticizing it,
a characteristic of realism in poetry. Yet my poems are not just instructive
rhymes. They are something more, with their own poetic voice. Their
changes in perspective make my poems more philosophical. Their clear
imagery makes them more intimate. The combination of the two encourages
personal feeling, a trademark of the Romantic Movement in poetry.
William Wordsworth, a founder of the Romantic Movement, said "poetry
is the spontaneous overflow of powerful feelings." May you have many
'Wordsworthian' moments as you read the poetry in
Perspectives of Nature Volume 2.
May the poetry found herein enlighten and inspire all who read or hear it.

— P. K.
March, 2020

Dedication

To Lilly,

who's always been supportive wife
in my not-always-normal life.

Table of Contents

Acknowledgements iv
Author's Introduction v
Sunrise Rhupunt 1
Spring Sonnet 3
Springs 5
Water 7
Mussels 9
Frog Calls 11
Tide Pools 13
Fireflies 15
Spider Webs 17
Hognose Snake 19
The Duel 21
Rare Sight 23
Row Your Crow 25
Poison Ivy 27
Gardening 29
Burn 31
The Tension Zone 33
Desert Pause 35
Sun 37
Full Moons 39
Equinoxes and Solstices 41
The Heavens 43
Lightning, Thunder 45
The Rock Cycle 47
Earth's Gems 49
Color Blind 51
Nettles 53
Gooseberries 55
Grasshopper Sparrow 57
Parenting 59
Motherhood 61
Index 63
About the Author 65
Photo Credits 66

Perspectives of Nature Volume 2

SUNRISE

The night is done,
new day begun,
first touch of Sun
provides us light.

By morning glow,
while Sun is low,
so starts the show
with lighting slight.

Each solar ray
ignites the day
and leads the way
within our sight.

Sky's reddish hue
next turns to blue,
starts life anew,
our future bright.

Notes

The preceding poem is a Welsh rhupunt in form and style.
The succeeding poem is an English sonnet in form and style.

Perspectives of Nature Volume 2

SPRING

Each Spring, the Earth knows not the day nor date,
  For Sun does not the numbered pages turn.
  Must we for warmer weather have to wait?
  Or has the daystar long enough to burn?

Ere sprinkles help the greening plants to bloom,
  The warm at night allows the same to grow
  And dainty buds detract from raining gloom
  Till pregnant streams with water overflow.

The minstrels sing an early daybreak song
  But unresponsive maidens send no love.
  To find a mate has taken far too long
With plaintive song of faithful mourning dove.

Cast out the thoughts of matters that you dread.
  A match appears with sunny days ahead.

Notes

Perched water table
   Saturated rock layer resting atop an impervious layer

Watershed
   An area of land that drains into a stream or river

Artesian ("ahr-TEE-zhen")
   Water that rises to the surface without being pumped

Aquifer ("AH-kwi-fer")
   A layer of saturated rock storing significant quantities of water

SPRINGS

Water seeping
Bedrock weeping

The rain sinks in until it's blocked,
within perched water-table locked.

Water dripping
Pebbles slipping

Erosion, some by gravity,
while water carves a cavity.

Water flowing
Streamlet growing

Ahead of movement ever down,
the soil of Life, first black, then brown.

Water spilling
Valley filling

then Time and Nature form the bed
of life-sustaining watershed.

Water trapped
Artesian tapped

To drive a pipe is only thing
that's needed to uncork this spring.

Water pressed
Landscape blessed

When aquifer is on a slope,
clear water rises, as does hope.

Notes

Aqueous ("AY-kwi-us")
   Taking place in or with water

Capillarity ("cap-ill-AIR-i-tee")
   The tendency in narrow tubes for liquids to rise or fall by surface tension

Vascular ("VASS-cue-lahr")
   A plant having cells specializing in moving water

Adhesion ("add-HEE-zhun")
   The tendency of water to cling to other substances

Cohesion ("co-HEE-zhun")
   The tendency of water to cling to itself

Perspectives of Nature Volume 2

WATER

Unique among the molecules of compounds world around,
 in liquid, gas, and solid states can water e'er be found.

All living things need H_2O, the chemical of life,
 to bathe reactions aqueous, assuaging thirsting strife.

Yet Life itself depends on traits of water physical;
 to help create and guide the surge of life force mystical.

Fresh water moves in lower plants by capillarity,
 but vascular in higher plants, a flower or a tree.

Adhesion and cohesion move fresh water through each plant,
 to transport Life's elixir to the places where it's scant.

And water shaped the faunal life that dwelt in ancient bays,
 archaic fish developed gills, employing water's ways.

To fish that live in waters fresh, dissolved O_2 gives breath;
 the floating ice and flow below, allow for cheating death.

Cold water holds more oxygen, the life-sustaining gas,
 so deeper in a frozen lake is where you'll find the bass.

Notes

Incurrent siphon ("INN-ker-rent SYE-fun")
    Tube-like tissue of a mussel that draws in water

Mantle
    Tissue lining the inside of a mussel's shell

Nacre ("NAY-ker")
    The inner layer of a mussel shell, mother of pearl

Glochidia ("gloh-KID-ee-uh")
    Tiny larval stage of a mussel

Sessile ("SESS-ill")
    Sedentary

MUSSELS

Without an eye, they watch Life's flow, the Mississippi clams.
At first, unbounded, then impounded by many locks and dams.

The yearly rhythm, flood and drought slows not the growth of shells,
but darkened rings denote the time of winter weather spells

Incurrent siphons bring in flow for mussels' life-long sip
to filter plankton, history from Mighty Mississip.

Beneath the mantle found within each shell that's made of lime,
is nacre lustrous, rich and smooth, sought after over time.

Ere plastics fastened all our clothes, pearl buttons were the trend,
this widespread use of mussel shells had put them near their end.

Then numbers rose, with types diverse, life cycle seemed secure:
eggs fertilized, glochidia, benign on host mature,

young mussels drop from fin or gill, beginning life anew.
The habitat that mussels need supports the host fish, too.

The latest pressures mussels feel are species introduced,
disrupting native mussels' lives, till numbers are reduced.

A mussel, sessile, anchors foot and moves itself a smidge,
Its body leaves a dragging trench, on either side a ridge.

Our eyes see zebra, quagga clams move at invasive speed.
Must slow them down to native pace, change something that they need.

Notes

Anurans ("ah-NER-anz")
   Frog and toad species

   Frog species appear in the poem in the order in which they generally sing in Wisconsin and the Upper Midwest.

FROG CALLS

In springtime, frogs begin to call, in ponds and wetter lands.
Before each call, their lungs inhale, their vocal sac expands.

This air is forced from sac to lungs, but never is it breathed.
The frog or toad tight lipped remains, its tongue is ever sheathed.

When air flows o'er their vocal chords, anurans sing the songs
comprising aural signatures, distinct from those of throngs.

The calls establish breeding grounds, the songs attract new mates;
frogs in a chorus pattern sing to see how each male rates.

The competition orderly, one frog and then the next;
each solo artist sings his song, described in coming text.

> The Wood Frogs make a croak from home
> While Chorus Frogs strum on a comb.
> The Peepers' peeps are next to spring,
> And sound like distant sleighbells ring.
> A Leopard Frog rubs tight balloon,
> a Pickerel then snores in tune.
> For many seconds trills a Toad,
> before Gray Treefrog's razzing flowed.
> then Cope's Gray treefrog buzzes back,
> as Cricket Frog two marbles clack.
> The Mink Frog trots on cobblestone
> and Green Frog twangs loose banjo tone.
> The last anuran call from lake
> is foghorn sound that bullfrogs make.

Notes

Echinoderms ("ee-KINE-oh-dermz")
  Marine invertebrates with spines on their skin (e.g. seastars)

Predaceous ("pree-DAY-shus")
  Predatory

Perspectives of Nature Volume 2

TIDE POOLS

In predawn light, ere curtains rose,
extreme environment we chose.
We found our seats to watch the shows
our spotlights shone, the action froze

Tide leaves some pools, more stages grow,
echinoderms where pools have flow.
At high tide, players live below,
but cling to rock when tide is low.

Exposed to sun, no chance to flee
predaceous birds, salinity.
Another stage, diversity
of colors, shapes, and pageantry.

Dark purple, pink, and yellow, green,
the strangest forms we'd ever seen,
A starfish odd, legs seventeen,
it takes a bow to end the scene.

A hermit crab has changed its shell
for matinee to play as well.
We watched more shows before the bell,
then waters rose and curtains fell.

Notes

Tracheoles ("TRAKE-ee-oles")
    Fine tubes in insects that allow gas exchange

Photuris
    A genus of firefly

FIREFLIES

When fireflies feel mating urge, males head to humid field
to cruise low vegetation haunts and signal lanterns wield.

Within these lamps, the chemicals react in mystery;
luciferin, luciferase make eerie light we see.

It's yellow, green, light red, or orange, one species even blue.
These magic 'flies withhold their light till dimness is their cue.

Then oxygen in tracheoles is fuel for bright, cool light;
without O_2, reaction stops and 'flies blend in with night.

The bits of light are flashed by males, in pattern of their kind;
in Smoky Mountains, unison, in Rockies, dark 'flies find.

When ladies of the lightning bugs see gents with finest glow,
they wink assent by flashing lights that match the male's show.

The femme fatale *Photuris* 'bug fools males of other kinds
by mimicking mate's blinking codes to eat lured 'bugs she finds.

Pairs trip the light fantastic while at Nature's bug-lit ball;
their messages mean naught to us, yet still they do enthrall.

Notes

Polymer
　Chemical compound with long molecules

Gossamer
　Filaments from a web spun by a spider

SPIDER WEBS

All spider types make protein silk, as liquid, pure and clear,
then load it in their spinnerets, the structures on their rear.

The polymer extruded firms as strong and tough as nails,
yet flexible, with tensile strength, the gossamer-made rails.

The architect first takes a chance, throws caution to the wind,
Letting go a test balloon with end of tether pinned.

The silk balloon, made sticky first, floats off on gentle breeze;
and then adheres to leaf or twig, is tightened then with ease.

Back and forth across the bridge to strengthen and inspect.
From anchor points, the frame is built in plane that stands erect.

First, central hub then radii are strung with silky strands.
Orb weavers next the spirals make, with tiny hook-like hands:

the dry lines first, from inside out, so spiders don't get caught,
then "capture spirals," outside in, with spider glue are fraught.

Orb weaver species make their webs in every shape and size.
Their beauty makes us marvel at the engineering prize.

So lovely and so intricate, it's hard for human thought
to fathom spiders' silk reuse; they eat what they have wrought.

Notes

Bufotoxic ("BOO-foh-tox-ick")
    Related to the poison found in a toad's skin and elsewhere in its body

HOGNOSE SNAKE

In early times, amphibians developed noxious skin;
for generations, toxic toads had evolution win.

By force of Life, not conscious thought, snakes started to withstand
the bufotoxic chemicals secreted from a gland.

But toads have yet another ploy to keep from being prey
of hognose snakes that hunger feel and catch a meal to slay.

Toads bloat themselves too big to eat, yet fight not always won;
the serpent has rear fangs to use to pierce, deflate – toad's done.

When hognose snakes the prey become, they differently behave;
their acts confuse their predators and scare away the brave.

This snake may flatten out its neck and feign a cobra hood;
behaviors shown by hognose snakes are neither bad nor good.

Their instinct makes them puff and hiss, the moves an adder makes.
Without intent, the serpent sounds like other venom snakes.

The final deed this snake may do is something 'possums try:
If faced with certainty of death, a hognose snake will 'die.'

With belly up, this snake will rest, might even droop its head.
but if it moves, will freeze again to show that it's still 'dead.'

Notes

Perspectives of Nature Volume 2

THE DUEL

So pleasant was the evening air and moonlit were the skies,
the crickets in the distance chirped, sweet fragrance on the rise.

The pipes were clogged, I washed by hand the night we had our duel.
I only wanted dishes clean and never to be cruel.

The wind picked up and rustled leaves, light rain began to fall,
an owl let out a warning hoot, and darkness cast a pall.

I washed the dishes, one by one, then put them in a rack,
next, took the dishpan through the house to empty from the back.

There was a sound, some feet away; I wondered what it was
because I know night noises not as well as Nature does.

I heaved the water anyway, but acted as a fool;
my toss became initial shot in very short-lived duel.

I saw no beast until it turned, then black back showed stripe white.
The skunk did not with rancor aim, yet squirted me with might.

Notes

Lupine (LOO-pine)
    Of or relating to wolves

Collar radio
    (or Radio collar) A tracking device worn by many of the 57 timber wolves living in Wisconsin at the time of the trip.

Perspectives of Nature Volume 2

RARE SIGHT

I headed north with travel friend, near Forest Nicolet.
We went to see the meteors, so drove up one clear day.

While up there we decided we'd each ride a rapid raft,
so made our way to river wild with rubber watercraft.

First drop of river threw me out, again and yet again.
Fourth time the charm, no body harm, put rafting in my ken.

But next came shallow river bed, where boulders stopped the boat
so that I had to leave the raft to help the vessel float.

Then roaring rapids, quickly passed, forced many daring swerves,
awareness peaked, my muscles taut, with frayed and tingling nerves.

The river flattened, water calmed, we moved into a cove.
With gentle waves along the shore, we saw a tiny grove.

Emerging from the little copse, it stood in fullest view
and lingered for a moment's time; my eyes saw something new,

like fifty-some around the state, worn collar radio.
Not husky dog, instead we saw endangered lupine show.

Notes

Murder
  A group of crows

Skeins (skaynz)
  Groups of geese that are flying (gaggles are groups of geese that are on the ground.)

Pate
  The forehead of a bird

This poem can be sung as a round

ROW YOUR CROW

Row, row, row your crow,
    murder in the air,
        big and black and menacing,
            and giving birds a scare.

                Honk, honk, honk your goose,
                  skeins in V's so high,
                      honking in migration to
                          and from the southern sky.

                Dip, dip, dip your flight,
              goldfinch undulate,
            "potato chip," is what you say,
        black cap upon your pate.

    Soar, soar, soar up high,
      wings in shallow "V",
   scanning with your turkey head,
dead carcasses to see.

Notes

Urushiol ("u-ROOSH-ee-awl")
The oily resin in poison ivy that can cause a reaction

POISON IVY

A mate came here from 'cross the Pond,
where grows no poison ivy frond,
which caused a hike to stretch our bond.

I showed the plant and took the lead,
but he did not my warning heed,
and brushed against the itching weed.

"If woody stems and leaflets three
on creeper, shoot, or vine you see,
the plant, and all it touched, do flee."

But next day no reaction seen
from ivy with red glossy sheen
or leaves of Summer, dull and green.

Again the next, no rash from plants.
Emboldened now, he took more chance,
the day a hole ripped in his pants.

Urushiol was wiped on thin
to newly unprotected skin
on rear of leg, above the shin.

Now twice exposed to ivy oil,
immunity began its toil
and made his fluids start to roil.

My English friend, intrepid Brit,
showed several days tremendous grit,
for all the while, he could not sit.

Notes

Perspectives of Nature Volume 2

GARDENING

Gardening's Goals
reap, eat,
repeat

Gardening's Gifts
peace of work
from
piece of work

Notes

Perspectives of Nature Volume 2

BURN

From planning the scorch to lighting the torch,
the burning goal is weed control
to help the fate of Nature's state.

With flame for breath, new life from death;
new green from black, when plants grow back.

Invasive plants lose growing chance
when combustive fuel is management tool;
weeds' edge deprive, so natives thrive.

The glowing light of plants at night
to ash will turn in evening burn.

Smoke from the blaze adds soot to the haze,
charred logs are smelled when flares are quelled.
then dowsing tames the crackling flames.

Smoldering birch in morning search
means dwindling heat, combustion complete.

The fire done, the battle won.

Notes

Perspectives of Nature Volume 2

THE TENSION ZONE

The State, Wisconsin, has a band, dividing south from north,
that Minnesota, Michigan, its neighbors, carry forth.

It shows where northern species grow in normal climate times
and marks the reach of southern plants in what are northern climes.

The range of more than hundred plants compiled to form the lines
on maps denoting Tension Zone; in Nature, shown by pines.

In region north of Tension Zone, some snows precede harsh cold,
whereas, in south, there's frozen ground ere bragging snows are told.

The climate of the Tension Zone controls the types of plants,
which then affect the faunal life and mammals seen by chance.

Above the line live porcupines, the star-nosed mole, and bears,
least chipmunks, woodland jumping mice, the lynx, and snowshoe hares.

To south, you'll find white-footed mice, opossum, eastern moles,
the ground squirrel marked with thirteen lines, and poorly-named pine voles.

The pine vole rarely enters pines, knows naught of Tension Zone.
It feels no tension, stress, or strain, and keeps a hungry tone.

Notes

DESERT PAUSE

While looking right as far as I could see,
I saw no living thing except for me.
On left I watched the west wind brush the land,
with nothing on the surface save for sand.
Behind, I left a trail of shifting grains,
made desolate by lack of living rains.
Before, stood dune and yet another dune,
bedazzling and stark against the noon.
Oppressive heat on every sandy knoll,
relenting not on path to final goal.
The searing Sun intensely at my heels,
I sifted sand with spokes of pedaled wheels.

Notes

Fusing
   The process of nuclear fusion

Supernova
   A star that is exploding

Sol ("sole")
   Our Sun

SUN

Within the furnace at its core,
our Sun does elemental chore

by fusing hydrogen to form
new helium in plasma storm.

Exploding forge will atoms bake,
to carbon and some others make.

Most heavy elements arise
with supernova stars' demise.

But not our Sun, its greatest grace
is radiation sent through space,

that powers weather, growth of plants,
affecting fauna's living chance,

providing and withdrawing Life,
the touch of Sun on Earth is rife.

In nightly dark, there is no Sol,
yet everywhere is solar role.

Notes

Corn
: the main grain of a country or region.

Perigee ("PARE-i-jee")
: The point in Earth's orbit around the Sun at which Earth is closest to the Sun (sometime in December)

Names in ALL CAPS
: are traditional Algonquin names for full moons.

Names in **bold**
: come from traditions and cultures other than Algonquin.

The Harvest Moon is not part of the monthly cycle of full moons because it is the full moon nearest to the Autumnal Equinox so can occur in September or October.

FULL MOONS

A spirit WOLF howls from the ages of **old,**
Full Moon after Yule with its treasures and gold.

When SNOW causes **hunger,** the moon never blue,
but may lack the "full" phase, opposing the new.

New WORMs work the soil and are eaten by **crows,**
with **Lenten** snow **crusty,** sweet maple **sap** flows.

Moss PINKs highlight **sprouting grass** growing so new.
Fish easy to catch and the robins' **eggs** blue.

More FLOWERs in May ease the **corn-planting** toil;
weeds eaten by cows add nutrition to soil.

Wild STRAWBERRYs flourish in **hot** moon of June,
in Europe it's **roses** that see the same moon.

BUCKs' antlers encased in soft velvet to show
and under the **thunder,** the **hay** stacks do grow.

The ancient fish, STURGEON, is easily speared;
when **fruit, grain, hay,** and **green corn** can be reared

CORN moon in September is not always maize,
main grain may be **barley** that livestock don't graze.

The HUNTER sees hunted in light of the night,
first **blood** then there's movement, tries not to lose sight.

A BEAVER cuts **frosty** trees, making a dome,
with offspring for helpers, the dome becomes home.

The COLD MOON reflected in long winter nights,
this perigee moon is the greatest of sights.

Notes

In the Northern Hemisphere:
 Summer Solstice – June 20, 21, or 22.
 Autumnal Equinox – September 22 or 23.
 Winter Solstice – December 20, 21, 22, or 23.
 Vernal Equinox – March 20 or 21.

Equinoxes and Solstices

Ecliptic is the path of Sol, the planets, and the Moon;
Sun closest in the wintertime and farthest out in June.

The tilt of Earth makes rays direct, for heating, this is prime;
and heat so gained, for months retained, does give us summertime.

That season starts when noontime Sun is highest in the sky;
at Summer Solstice, several days, our nearby star stands high.

Each day for months, Sol does not rise as high as day before;
till daytime Sun equates the Night, which then grows more and more.

At Equinox, the dwindling Sun passes o'er Equator;
we set our clocks as darkness creeps, no longer hour later.

The shortened days still shorter turn, till nearly reaching Yule,
their heaters on, most people give, but never lumps of fuel.

On Winter Solstice comes the gift, awaited for a year;
the days are longer, bit by bit, in coldest months, some cheer.

At Vernal Equinox we plan how soon we'll feign rebirth.
so that on Summer Solstice we'll start harvest from the Earth.

Notes

Epicycles
    Circles imagined along planets' orbits that helped to describe observations better mathematically.

Ptolemy is pronounced with a silent "P."

For this poem, Tycho Brahe's name is pronounced as my professor pronounced it, "tee-koh brah-hay."

Perspectives of Nature Volume 2

THE HEAVENS

Sumerians, Akkadians, four thousand years ago,
Looked up and saw in pitch black skies a starlit picture show.

As Taurus, Leo, Scorpio, and Capricorn first cast,
did usher in the seasons four and told of stories past.

The cycle of their zodiac, which moved around the sky,
was passed along to ancient Greeks, with explanation bye.

So Aristotle placed the stars and planets that were known
upon concentric crystal spheres, themselves were never shown.

With epicycles, Ptolemy explained how planets moved;
For more than fourteen hundred years he could not be disproved.

Then Tycho Brahe smashed the orbs and epicycles, too.
The planets traced elliptic arcs, Johannes Kepler knew.

They moved around the Sun, not Earth, Copernicus was sure.
In Galileo's telescope were moons of Jupiter.

The telescope that Hubble dreamed was built by modern tech,
but based on bygone scientists and answered to their beck.

Notes

Potential difference
: The difference in electric charge that causes electrons to flow.

Ion ("EYE-on")
: An atom or group of atoms that has lost or gained one or more electrons.

Perspectives of Nature Volume 2

LIGHTNING

The turbulence of wind aloft in mighty thunderclouds
may strip from upper particles their charged electron shrouds

to leave in higher parts of clouds a charge that's positive,
at odds with lower parts of clouds with ions negative.

Potential difference in the cloud may cause electron flow;
this lightning type, by name of "sheet," can make the whole cloud glow.

If flow of charge is cloud to cloud, and seen, but never heard,
the discharge has another name, "heat lightning" is the word.

Most dangerous and damaging is lightning cloud-to-ground,
when pent-up charge in lower clouds sends leaders earthward bound.

Descending pathways step by step, these leaders act as scouts
to meet with streamers rising up along the shortest routes.

Together form returning stroke of all the static charge,
in what we see as lightning bolt that's luminously large.

In mountaintops, the bolts intense cause "elves" and "jets" and "sprites,"
but clouds that cause all lightning strikes have ice within their heights.

With energy more powerful and crack extremely loud,
some lightning strikes the other way, from ground up to the cloud

THUNDER

A lightning strike is hotter than the Sun
and lights the sky as much, but then is done.

The air around the bolt expands so fast,
it's heard as though a shock wave from a blast.

If vertical, the lightning sounds a crack;
less upright, thunder rolls on broken track.

The time that lapses, light till slower sound,
is used to measure where a storm is found.

Five Mississippi's counted are a mile
and make one more perceptive for a while.

Notes

Obsidian ("ahb-SID-ee-an")

Lithogenic stock
  Rock-producing material

Plutonic
  Intrusive; occuring when molten magma is forced into pre-existing rock.

Gneiss ("nice")

Perspectives of Nature Volume 2

THE ROCK CYCLE

≈ Igneous ≈

When magma deep in Earth is warmed,
intrusive igneous is formed.
Time slowly cools the molten rock
to minerals in position lock,
but molten rock not deep below
cools quickly, makes a lava flow.
Eruptions give off noxious gas,
obsidian, volcanic glass.

≈ Metamorphic ≈

Enormous pressure brought to bear
on heated rocks already there
that change to metamorphic rock
with denser lithogenic stock.
Plutonic granite turns to gneiss
with layers flat that do not slice.
Among the oldest rocks on Earth,
four billion years since geo-birth.

≈ Sedimentary ≈

Third type is rock from sediment
that's held together by 'cement.'
The sediments of sand and mud
turn shale and sandstone under flood.
As seas advanced and then withdrew,
the lime from shells reduced and grew,
so lives of shellfish can be read
in size of every limestone bed.

Notes

Chalcedony ("kal-SED-oh-nee")
   A form of quartz

Saturated
   As much of a substance dissolved as possible

Solutes ("SAHL-yutes")
   The substances being dissolved

Ovoid
   Egg-shaped

Moganite
   Mineral that forms around agates.

Silica
   Silicon dioxide (SiO_2). A common mineral that can be of different colors, depending on the impurities present

Nucleation points ("new-klee-AY-shun)
   Points of origination for coloration

EARTH'S GEMS

Geodes

In secret, Nature lays her eggs, rocks lacking artistry;
no decorations on their shells of quartz chalcedony.

Instead, their shells, when broken, show the mineral gifts inside,
from solutions saturated, there grew solutes that since dried.

A crystal palace lies within each dingy ovoid stone;
amid the gems, a seat unseen for Mother Nature's throne.

Each floor and wall with jewels bedecked, on ceilings, chandeliers.
The other geodes, still intact, unopened through the years.

Agates

As gases of the early Earth escaped its lava flows,
then Time made cooling bubble frames and fashioned studios

with outer walls of moganite, which looked like normal stones,
but inside, workshops stocked with gel-like silica for tones

to paint small frescoes on the walls at nucleation points,
adhering there with micro-crystal curvy fiber joints.

More coats, more coats till Time is done; the agate filled, unique.
When hewn, it shows the banding that the agate-hunters seek.

Notes

Espial ("ess-PILE")
  Espying, catching sight of.

COLOR BLIND

With man-made hues, I'm color-blind; I do not know the tints
of fabrics in the fashion world or tinctures found in chintz.

I know not French nor heraldry, so not the color vert.
What I see best are Nature's tones and different shades of dirt.

Some tinges that I do not know are taupe and puce and dun;
they're artificial stylish dyes, made indoors, not in sun.

Sienna brown, I never know, if yellowish or red.
Cerise is red that's light and clear whenever it is said.

Not so for "lake," a word for red that means deep water blue
or "madder," yellow-flowered plant, that's also reddish hue.

And "fallow" means a resting field, but also yellow shade;
I've seen this color many times, as fields begin to fade.

Cerulean is blue I know, a warbler streaked on back.
A bunting male looks indigo yet pigment only black.

I see the light, reflected blue; it always makes me smile:
not color-blind, I see what's hid – the bunting blue espial.

Notes

NETTLES

One day while at the garden bed, when I was just a child,
my father tried to teach me weeds encroaching from the wild.

"Come over, Son, and feel this plant, with nettle for a name."
My tender fingers burned and itched, as if too near a flame.

Much later, while a nature guide, I studied nettle plants,
which have the formic acid found in painful biting ants.

The hollow hairs of stem and leaf break off and then inject
their acid into skin laid bare, where clothes do not protect.

Laportea, wood-nettle, grows in shaded, wooded stands,
but stinging nettles, *Urtica,* in open, vacant lands.

With cooking, nettles lose their sting, are safe and edible.
Their simmered leaves and cooking broth each taste incredible.

While leading hikes, I always warned to touch no nettles raw,
nor eat them without cooking first, lest feel a throbbing maw.

One day while hiking on his trails, I told this to my dad,
who bested me a second time, ate nettles and was glad.

Notes

Many gooseberry (*Ribes*) species have no prickles on the berry, but the shrub in our yard was *Ribes cynosbati,* called prickly gooseberry or dogberry, which had them.

Perspectives of Nature Volume 2

GOOSEBERRIES

One day while swinging happily, when I was just a lad,
I heard him call from 'cross the lawn, so ran to be with Dad.

"They're ready, Son," he smiled at me. I peered around his knee
then stared in horror at the shrub, "There's prickers!" was my plea.

Dad said the berries tasted good and gave me some to try.
I paused and backed a step or two and then began to cry.

I whined and whimpered endlessly; I did not want to eat
the pea-sized fruits with pointy parts, though Dad called them a treat.

He said again they would not hurt; my heart and mind were torn.
He ate a few to prove them safe, I touched the longest thorn.

"The fresh new spines are soft, not sharp," said Dad's assuring voice.
I sniffled once then wiped my tears, looked up and made my choice.

The unripe fruits had tasty crunch, two acids made them tart.
Dad always knew I'd say someday, "I loved them from the start."

Notes

Bucolic ("byu-KAH-lick")
   Pastoral, rural

Heifers ("heff-erz")
   Young female bovines that have not yet calved.
   (Cows already have calved.)

GRASSHOPPER SPARROW

My dad grew up on sandy farm in center of our state,
bucolic lessons in his heart, experiences great:

truck farming spuds and roofing barns with ice cream as a goal.
He'd beat the heat, once chores were done, down at the swimming hole.

His lessons in biology were making heifers cows,
He learned the birds while shearing sheep before he let them browse.

It always seemed he knew the birds and mammals that we saw.
With mentor set, my goal was clear – know birds without a flaw.

One day he pointed in the sky, said "nighthawk" with a smile.
"How do you know? What makes it so?" He said, "I guess, its style."

Not learning from his farm-taught ways, I gave to them a pass.
Instead, I thought, while off at school, I'd take a birding class.

In May one year, while home from school, we visited a park.
I wished to show him birds I'd learned, like cuckoos and a lark.

When we saw jays and chickadees, my dad was in his prime,
but warblers, thrushes, vireos would stump him every time.

Most birds we saw were new to him, I didn't want to chide,
but finished with a bird ID that might have hurt his pride.

When something buzzed, my father said, relief upon his face,
"At least I know what made that sound – grasshopper in this place."

I knew the call and whirled around to see the birding treat,
Grasshopper *sparrow* on a stump, my triumph bittersweet.

Notes

PARENTING

Our children die a thousand deaths,
  but other mammals, one,
for parents yearn for bygone times
  ere childhood days were done.

We watch our children grow and learn,
  are proud but saddened, too;
  once curious, naive, and dear;
    the loss of these we rue.

We teach them lessons, guide their lives,
  which starts a wistful flood
of thoughts nostalgic that we feel
  about our flesh and blood.

These memories remind us that
  our children's youth must end,
to be replaced by grown-up souls,
  adults we need not tend.

But mammals never mark the dates
  their offspring grow, mature.
Their young live life until they die,
  a mass of flesh and fur.

Notes

Perspectives of Nature Volume 2

MOTHERHOOD

En route one morn to birding place, where mighty river flowed,
saw I bare shell of hollow tree, collapsed upon the road.

While dragging off the bark-less hull, I saw a broken egg,
then two then three then more than four, then duck with injured leg.

The hen had found an egg intact and clutched it in her wing;
she shivered by the lifeless egg, but instinct made her cling.

I scooped the female wood duck, for she couldn't walk that far;
and placed her in a cardboard box in front seat of my car.

I ran the heat to keep her warm and drove her toward the shore,
Next, waited for two passing trains, one stopped and went no more.

The train that stopped held railroad men, who checked the crossing gate.
Determined then to reach the shore, I seized from them her fate.

The bird, I carried o'er the tracks and set in sunny place.
She paused at length, near water's edge; concern spread 'cross my face:

the hope, not hers, but mine alone, for outcome that was good.
She bolted in, and claimed her chance at future motherhood.

Index

About the Author 65
Acknowledgements iv
Author's Introduction v
Burn 31
Color Blind 51
Desert Pause 35
Earth's Gems 49
Equinoxes and Solstices 41
Fireflies 15
Frog Calls 11
Full Moons 39
Gardening 29
Gooseberries 55
Grasshopper Sparrow 57
Hognose Snake 19
Lightning 45
Motherhood 61
Mussels 9
Nettles 53
Parenting 59
Poison Ivy 27
Rare Sight 23
Row Your Crow 25
Spider Webs 17
Spring Sonnet 3
Springs 5
Sun 37
Sunrise Rhupunt 1
The Duel 21
The Heavens 43
The Rock Cycle 47
The Tension Zone 33
Thunder 45
Tide Pools 13
Water 7
Photo Credits 66

Also by Paul Košir

About the Author

The scientifically romantic nature poetry of Paul Košir has its academic roots in his nine years as a student at the University of Wisconsin-Madison. There he earned bachelor's degrees in math, natural science, and history. In 2010 he received a master's degree in natural resources and environmental education
from UW-Stevens Point.

The experiential poetry was drawn from his twelve years as the naturalist at Wyalusing State Park near Prairie du Chien, Wisconsin. He also drew on this background to write articles
for *Wisconsin Natural Resources*
and *La Crosse Magazine*
and to publish the book *Wyalusing History*.

Košir has taught biology, physical science, and math
at the high school level; and earth science, biology,
and environmental issues at the college level. As a naturalist, he taught all ages about nature through hikes, programs, and displays, something he still does occasionally as a volunteer.

Born in Milwaukee, Košir now lives in La Crosse with his wife and their two sons. He enjoys writing, hiking, bird-watching, gardening, traveling, and visiting relatives.

Photo Credits

Front Cover
Hermit crab found by the author's wife in
Olympic National Park and photographed by the author.

Back Cover
Sea star (star fish) found by the author's older son in
Olympic National Park and photographed by the author.

www.ingramcontent.com/pod-product-compliance
Lightning Source LLC
Chambersburg PA
CBHW052121110526
44592CB00013B/1700